Conrad K. Butler

Why is milk white and the sky blue?

Why is it raining?

Well, imagine the clouds in the sky having a massive water balloon fight. These clouds are fluffy friends filled with tiny drops of water. When these water droplets get together and decide to team up, they form a heavy, soggy alliance that can't float in the air anymore. It's like a super exclusive raindrop club, and when they've had enough fun in the clouds, they dive down to the ground as rain. So, next time you see raindrops, just know that it's the clouds having the ultimate splashdown party!

Why is the sky blue?

Well, it's like the sun is a magical rainbow flashlight, and it shoots out seven awesome colors. But here's the funny part – the air is a bit of a color bouncer. It only lets the super cool blue color join the party and dance in the sky. So, when you look up, you're basically seeing the sky doing its favorite blue dance. It's like the air saying, 'Blue, you're the star here!' So, next time you spot that blue sky, just know it's the coolest color having the best dance party up there!

Why does a rainbow appear?

It's like having a secret code to find a colorful treasure in the sky! Imagine the sun as your flashlight. When raindrops join the party after a bit of rain, they become like sparkling crystals, catching the sunlight. Now, here's the cool part: to spot the rainbow magic, you turn your back to the sun and face where the rain is falling. It's like playing hide-and-seek with colors! The sun sends its light through the raindrops, and they're fantastic little reflectors, bouncing the light back to you in seven amazing colors. So, when you see a rainbow, it's like nature's way of winking and saying to you: 'Hey, look at this beautiful surprise I made just for you!'.

Why do we get goosebumps?

Well, it's like having a built-in superhero power! Imagine your body as a cozy little castle, and when it feels a chilly breeze, it's time for the invisible cloak to save the day. When the air gets a bit nippy, your hair becomes like tiny knights standing up to protect you. They create a warm barrier, huddling together to keep the cold at bay. It's like your body's way of saying, 'Fear not, brave knight! I've got this.' So, the next time you get goosebumps, just know it's your invisible cloak gearing up to keep you snug and warm in your own little fortress!

Why do we feel pain?

Well, it's like having an alarm system in our bodies! Imagine you're a brave explorer, and pain is your trusty sidekick, warning you about potential dangers. Even though pain isn't exactly a party guest, it's a lifesaver. When something hurts, it's your body's way of saying, 'Hey, something's not right here! Pay attention!' It's like a little red flag waving to grab your attention. So, the next time you feel pain, think of it as your body's superhero hotline, letting you know it's time to be careful or call in the expert (like your grown-ups or a doctor) to help fix things. Pain may not be fun, but it's your body's way of being the best sidekick it can be!

Why do we pee?

It's like our body's little cleaning mission! Imagine your body as a cool factory that processes all the drinks you enjoy. Now, some drinks bring awesome stuff that your body needs, while others bring in things it doesn't. All those 'extras' end up in a special storage tank called the bladder, which is like a hidden container in your lower belly. When this container gets full, your body sends you a little message saying, 'Hey, time to let go of the stuff we don't need!' And that's when you visit the bathroom. So, peeing is your body's way of staying tidy and making sure you only keep the good stuff. It's like being a superhero for cleanliness - Captain Clean, at your service!

Why is the lion the king of animals?

Well, it's like nature's own rockstar! Lions are like the tough champions of the wild because they're great at playing tag – they run super fast! Imagine lions as the cool athletes of the animal Olympics, zooming across the grasslands like speedy runners. And oh, that roar! It's not just any sound; it's like their way of saying, 'Hey, I'm the ruler here!' It's a bit like a lion's royal microphone, making everyone stop and listen. So, when it comes to being tough and making a grand entrance, lions are the true kings of the animal kingdom.

Why do chickens have wings but don't fly?

It's like having a feathered friend who prefers hopping to soaring! Imagine hens as the cozy, downy teddy bears of the barnyard. While they can flutter a bit above the ground, their wings are like gentle whispers, not jet engines. You see, their bodies are like little gravity magnets, and their wings, though charming, are like delicate whispers in the breeze. So, when you see a chicken, just know it's a fluffy friend who likes keeping its feet on the ground, exploring the farmyard with a skip and a hop. Flying? That's for the feathered superheroes in the sky!

Why do planes leave white streaks in the sky?

It's like a magical sky art show! Picture planes as speedy paintbrushes with warm engines. As they zoom by, their engines leave behind an invisible trail, just like whispers in the air. Now, guess what? Tiny, unseen water droplets in the sky decide to join the fun. The engine's warmth is like a wizard's spell, making these invisible droplets come together in a cloud ribbon dance. It's the airplane's way of saying, 'Look at the sky art I made!' But, like a game of peek-a-boo, after a little while, the cloud ribbon decides to take a solo and disappears. So, when you see those white streaks, it's the sky sharing the airplane's secret art show with you.

Why do stars shine?

Well, think of stars as the cosmic nightlights in the sky, each one a giant fireball throwing a radiant glow. Even though they seem small, it's because they're having a game of hide-and-seek from way, way up above. So, when you look up on a clear night, you're witnessing a massive celestial bonfire, and those twinkling stars are like friendly fireflies in the vast cosmic backyard. It's the universe's way of saying, 'Hey, check out the magical show I've got going on up here!

Why do grandma and grandpa have gray hair?

It's like their hair is whispering secrets of wisdom! Our hair gets its color from a special paint called pigment, and when we're little, we have lots of it, making our hair look like vibrant rainbows. But as we grow older, the pigment takes a break, and the hair decides to tell a different story - a tale of experiences and knowledge. So, when you see grandma and grandpa with their silver hair, it's like they've transformed into magical wizards, carrying the enchanting stories of a life well-lived. Their gray hair is like the universe's way of giving them a crown of wisdom!

Why is the grass green?

Imagine every little grass blade as a mini artist with a special color palette. The secret ingredient for its green masterpiece is a cool thing called chlorophyll – it's like the grass's own magical paint! Chlorophyll works like sunshine magnets, catching sunbeams and turning them into that awesome green color. So, when you see a grassy field, it's like nature saying, 'Look at this fantastic green garden I painted just for you!' The grass is like a living carpet of color, making the outdoors look super cool and vibrant. Nature is the best artist, isn't it?

Why do animals have tails?

It's like nature's way of giving them a handy tool kit! Imagine tails as animal superheroes – not with capes, but with tails that can do all sorts of cool tricks. Tails help animals keep their balance, like a built-in tightrope, especially when they're jumping or climbing. And here's the fun part: tails are like animal talkers! Some animals use them to say, 'Hey, I'm happy!' or 'Watch out, I'm excited!' Tails are like the special, swishy language animals use to tell us how they're feeling!

Why do we need two nostrils?

Well, it's like having a fantastic smell team inside your nose! Think of them as nature's dynamic duo – one on the right and one on the left. Having two helps us sniff out all the amazing scents in the world. One nostril might be the superhero breather, doing the heavy lifting when we take big whiffs, while the other takes a little break. And guess what? They switch roles! It's like a tag-team match for your nose. So, when you catch the delightful aroma of your favorite food or the sweet scent of flowers, give a little nod to your trusty double-nostril squad.

Why is milk white?

It's like a yummy magic trick by nature! Inside milk, there's a special ingredient called cream, sort of like milk's superhero. This cream is full of teeny, invisible fat droplets. When these droplets hang out in milk, they catch the sunlight and twirl it around, turning milk into a beautiful, snowy white. So, when you pour a glass of milk or pour it on your cereal, think of it as sipping on a glass of nature's delightful and sunlit surprise.

Where do holes in cheese come from?

It's like cheese has a secret bubbly party going on! Imagine cheese as a cozy home for friendly bacteria. These little buddies love to snack on the cheese and produce gas as a thank-you gift. As the cheese ages, these gas bubbles get trapped inside, creating those fun holes. So, when you see holey cheese, it's like discovering a cheese bubble fiesta – the more bubbles, the merrier!

Why does one cry when cutting an onion?

It's like the onion is playing a little trick on us! Onions have a superpower called sulfur. When we cut them, they release tiny sulfur gas molecules into the air. These mischievous molecules make their way to our eyes and team up with tears, creating a bit of a ticklish sensation. So, when you're chopping onions, it's like having a playful onion party where the onions want to make you laugh with tears. It's the onion's way of saying, 'Hey, I might make you cry a bit, but I promise I'll add lots of flavor to your yummy meal!' So, next time an onion makes you tear up, just remember it's a little kitchen comedian!

Why do we have day and night?

Well, it's like our Earth has its own fantastic light switch! You see, our planet loves to spin around, and when it turns toward the Sun, it's daytime - time for adventures, play, and sunshine hugs. But when we spin away, it's nighttime, and Earth takes a bit of a cosmic nap in the shadowy corner.

Day and night happen because our planet can't resist twirling around, sharing the Sun's warmth with everyone. So, it's like Earth saying, 'Let's have a little dance with the Sun and then cozy up for a good night's rest.' It's the Earth's way of making sure every day is a perfect blend of fun and a good night's sleep!

Check also:

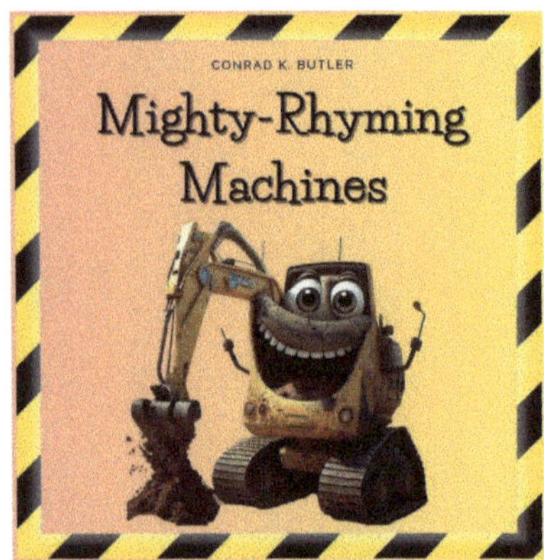

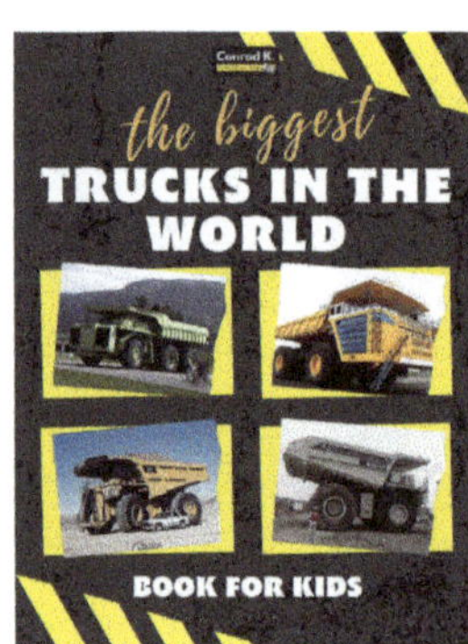

and much more!